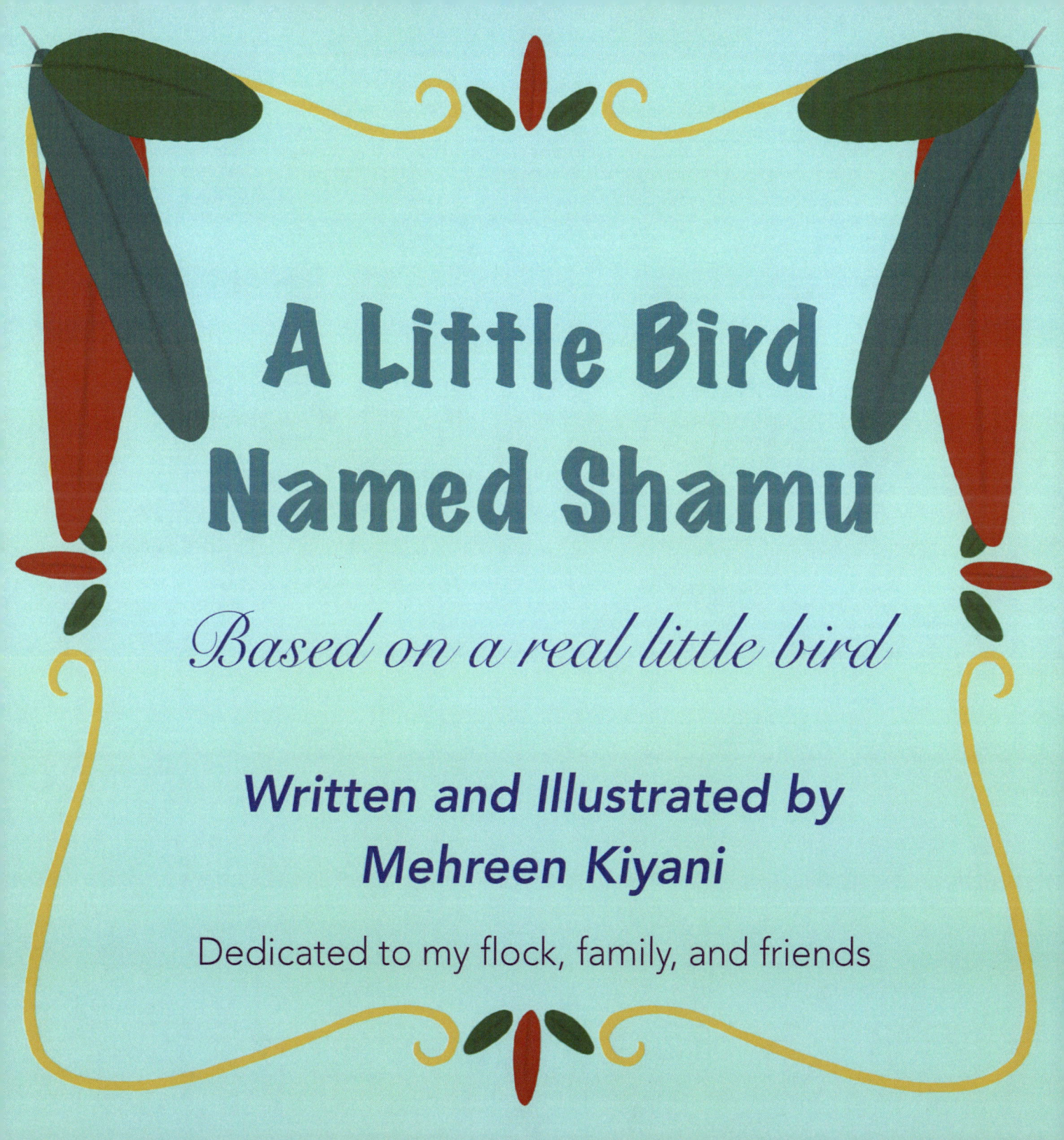

A Little Bird Named Shamu

Based on a real little bird

Written and Illustrated by
Mehreen Kiyani

Dedicated to my flock, family, and friends

I am a little bird named Shamu. The type of bird I am is called a green cheek conure, because I have fluffy green cheeks.

I was a little baby bird when I met my mom at a pet store. She took me home and we became a family.

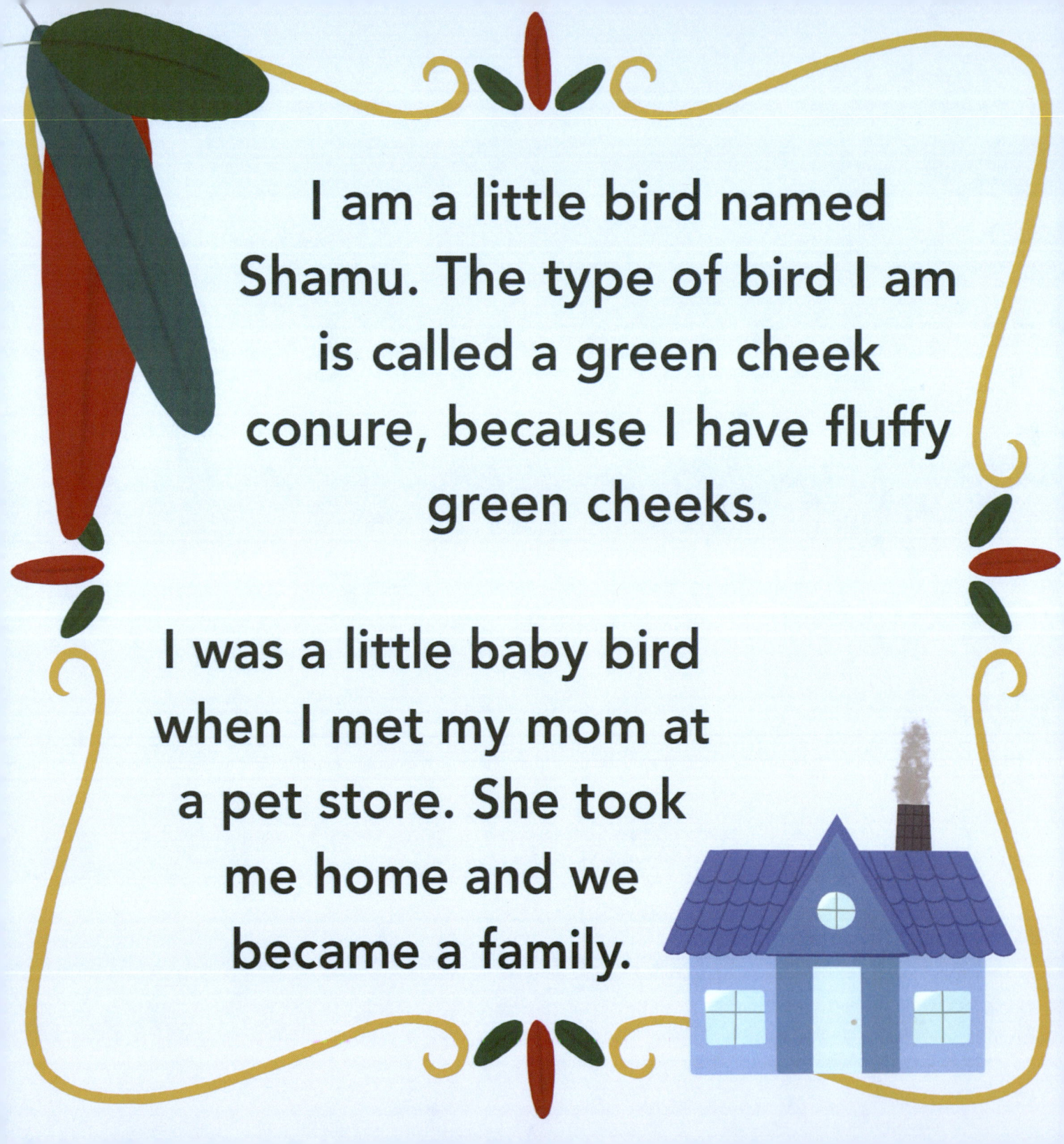

My mom doesn't look like me. She's a lot bigger. She has no feathers, wings, or a beak, but I still like her.

She gives me hugs and kisses. She plays with me. And she gives me my favorite snacks.

That's me!

There are a lot of types of food I like. I like eating fruits, seeds, and pellets. It is important for me to eat nutritious food so I can be strong and healthy.

My most favorite snack is an apple. I love when my mom cuts them into little pieces for me to eat.

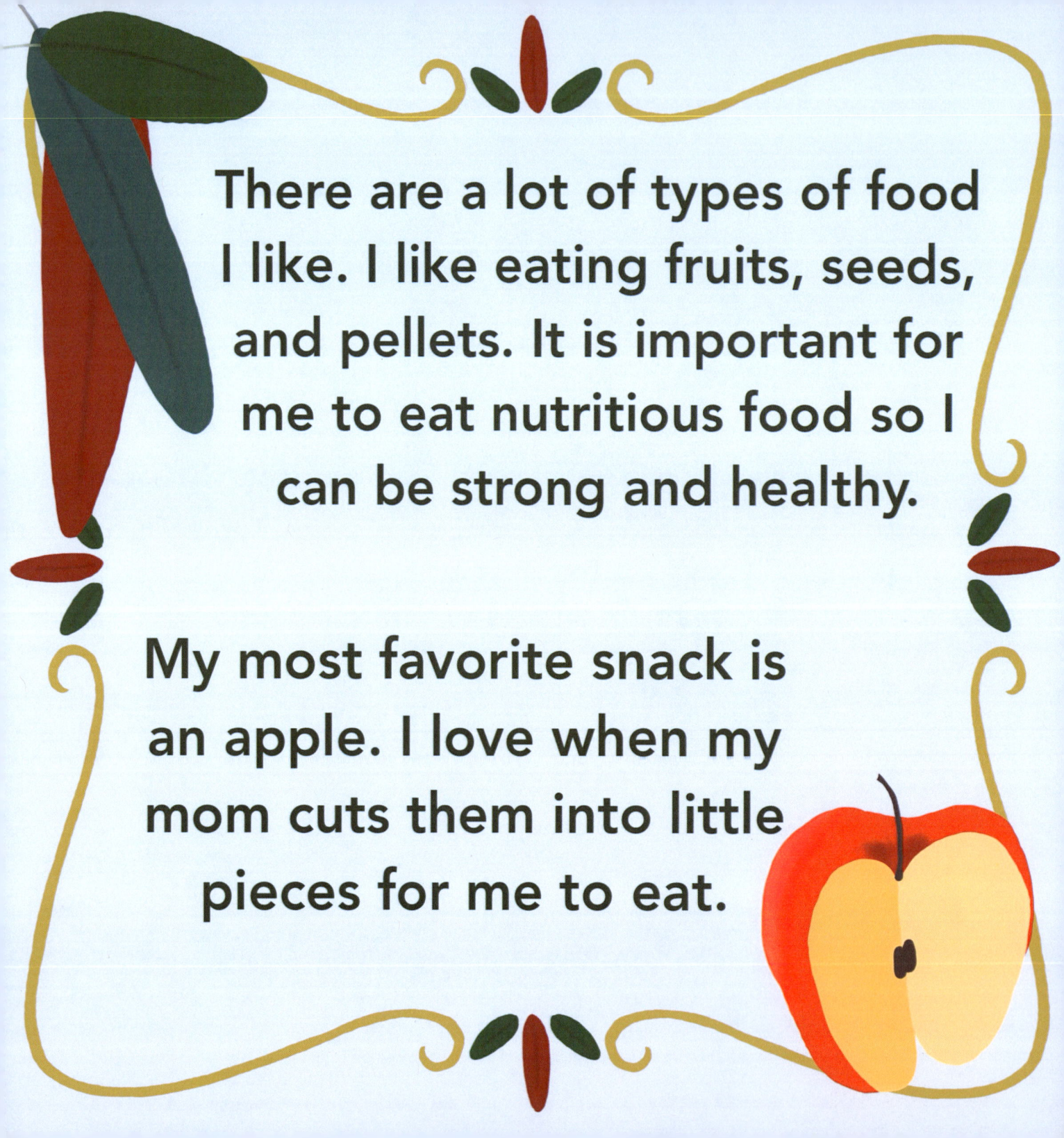

I am a great dancer. I like dancing to all types of music. I love music that is cheerful and has a fun rhythm.

I practice my dancing a lot so I can be the best bird dancer.

Working hard is important to achieve my goal.

I also like playing with my toys. I have a lot of different kinds of toys.

I have colorful balls and shiny bells. Some of my toys are big and some of them are small.

They are all very fun to play with and help me stay active.

My mom calls me her little prince. That means I am very important and special.

I can do whatever I want. I get a lot of gifts and treats almost every day.

Everyone adores me and makes sure I am happy. For a long time, I was the center of attention.

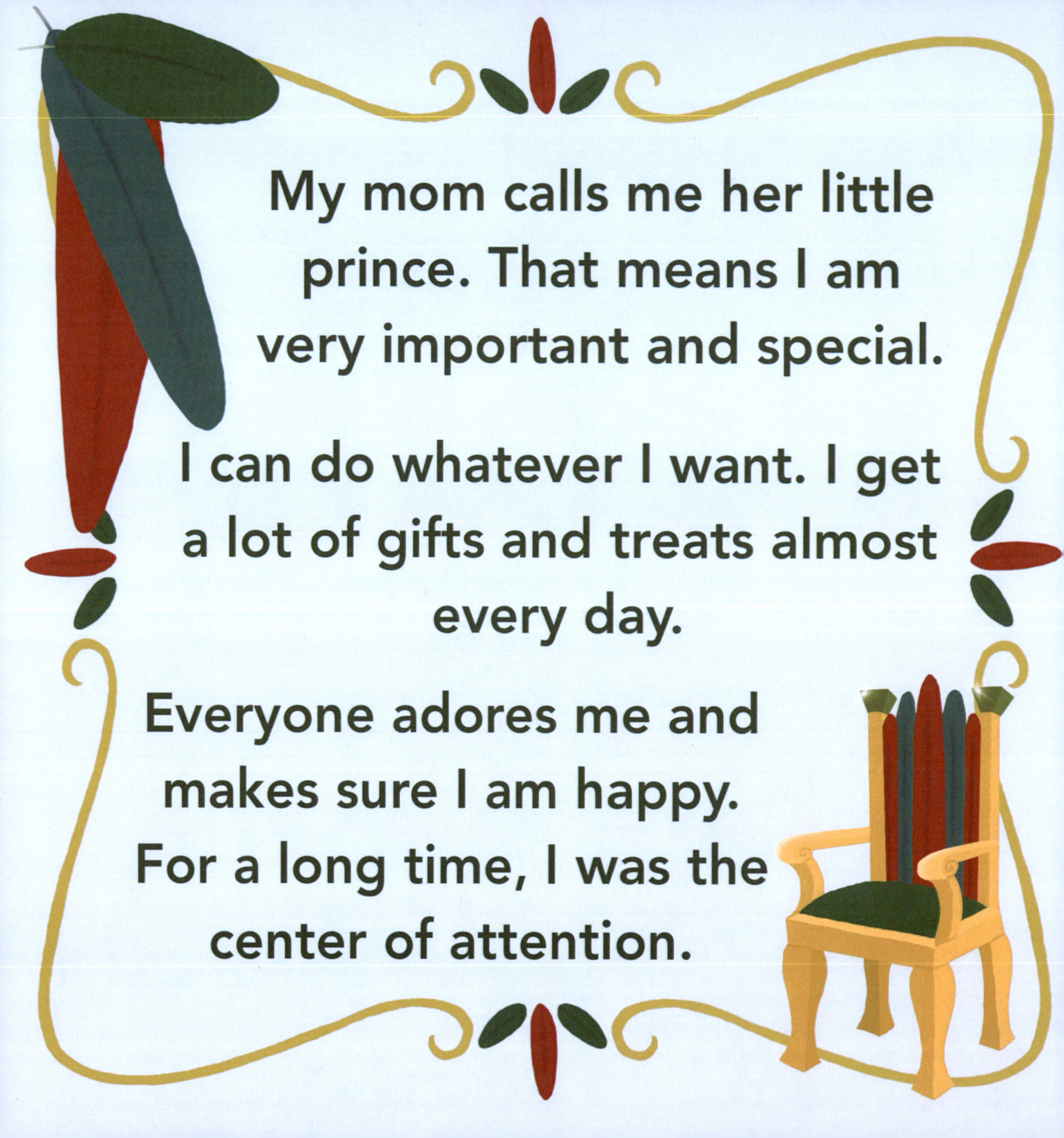

About two years after I met my mom, she introduced me to my little brother. His name is Pebbles.

After he came home, I had to share my toys and treats, and I wasn't the center of attention anymore.

But I was still happy to have a brother and we became best friends.

Sometimes Pebbles and I get angry at each other and fight. Then, we stop talking to each other for a while.

Eventually, we forgive each other. Even if he makes me upset sometimes, our friendship is still very important to me.

Sometimes Pebbles likes to fly around our home. He flaps his wings up and down really hard and sores up very high.

He can fly up to the ceiling and down to the floor. He can fly to the left or to the right. He can get to places quickly and easily.

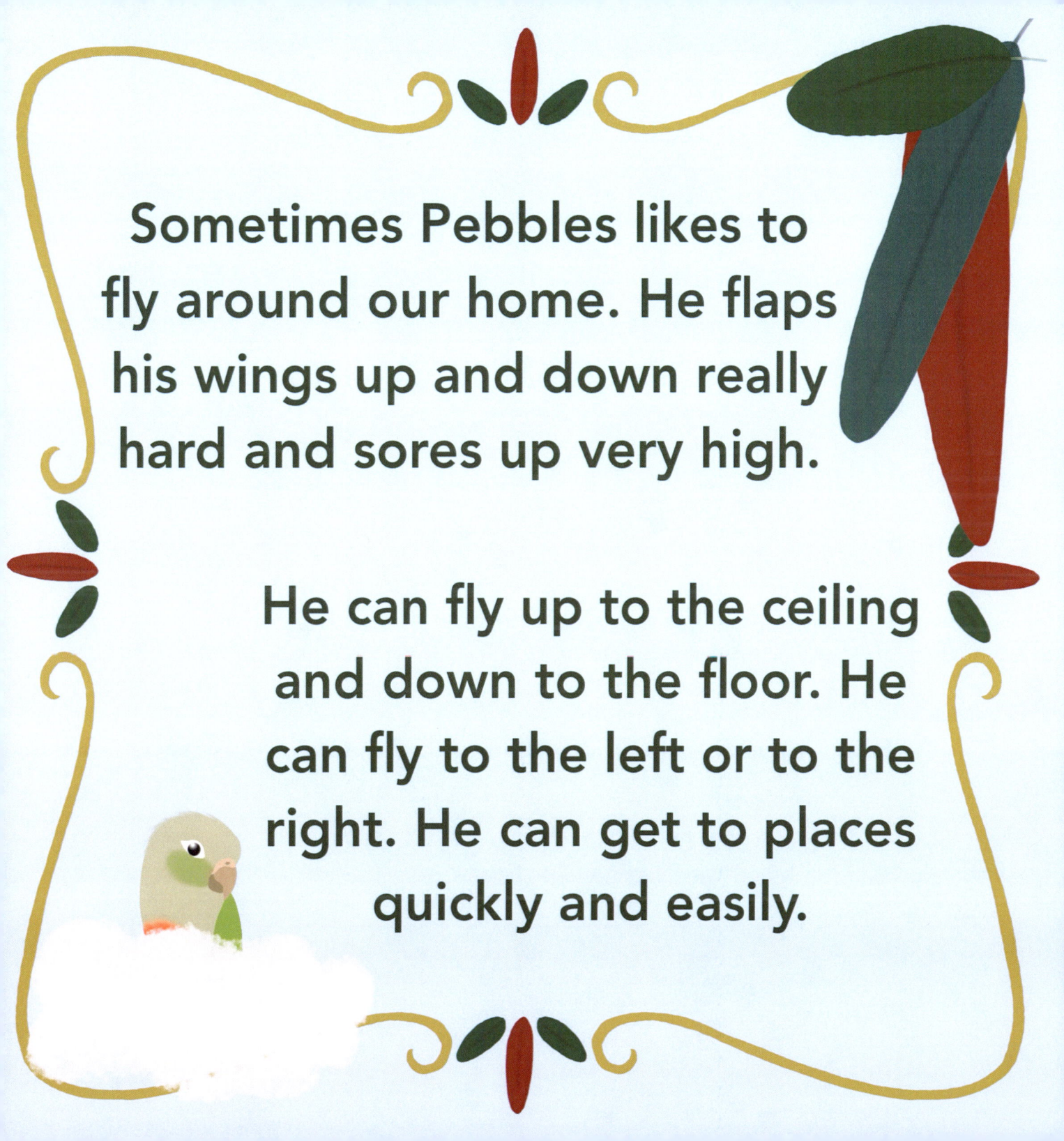

I can't fly like Pebbles. I hurt my right wing as a baby before I met my mom. If I try to flap my wings, I fall to the ground.

It is a lot harder for me to get to places, because I can't fly like other birds. I need to be creative to get to where I want to go.

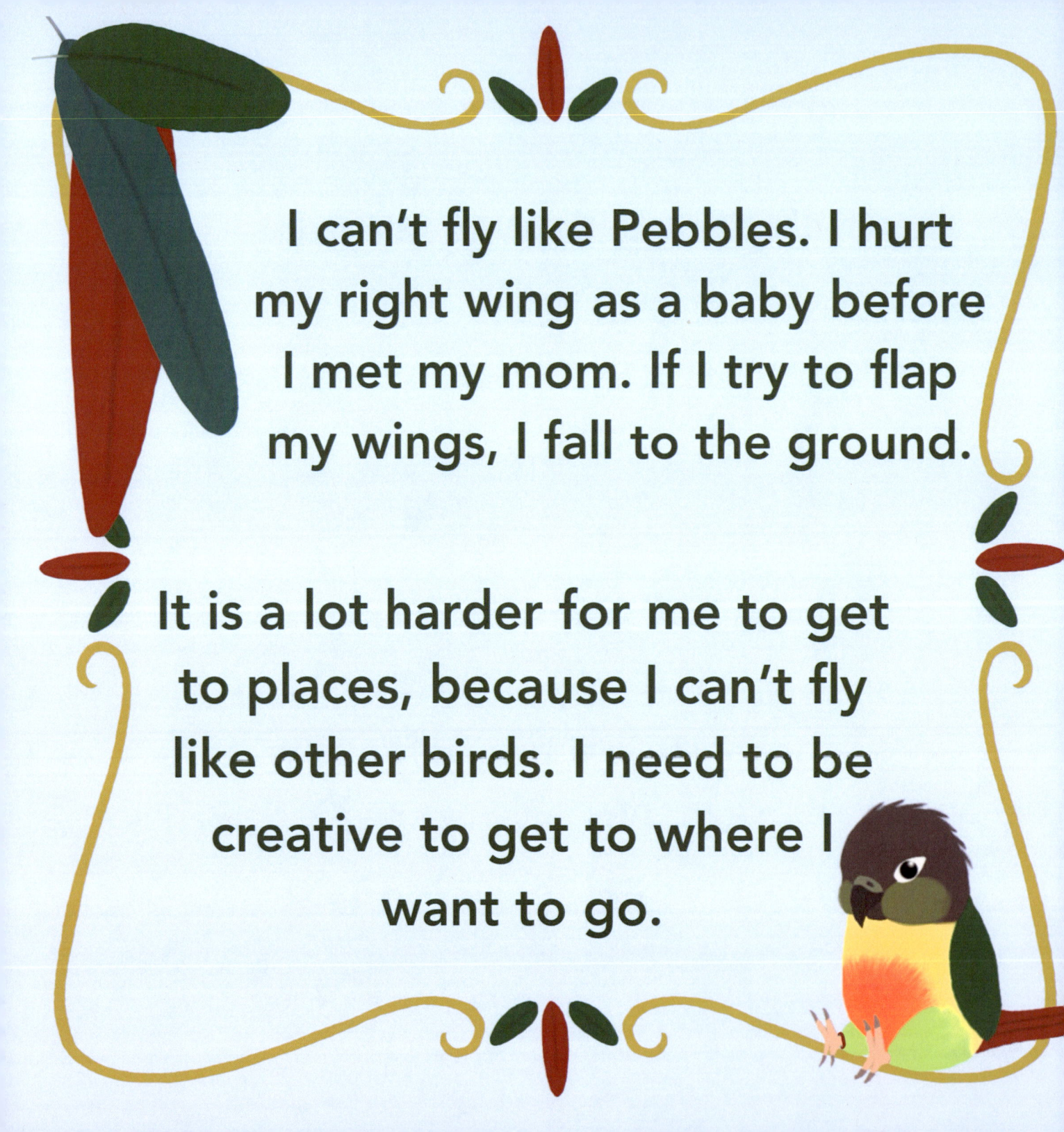

Sometimes if we notice treats that got left on a table, Pebbles immediately flies to the table and starts eating the treats right away.

My little brother is not always good at sharing, so I have to be clever to figure out a way to get there quickly before all of the treats are gone.

I can climb really well.

And I can jump very far.

My mom tells me I am very smart and she is proud of me. Even though I am different from other birds, I am talented and awesome in my own unique way.

Some things may not be as easy for me, but I always stay positive and am still a very happy little bird.

Author's Note:

I adopted Shamu in October 2015 when he was six months old. He was named using the combination of the first letters of my siblings' and my names: "Sh" for my sister, "M" for me, and "U" for my brother.

Shamu has always been very social and playful. Having birds is a lot of responsibility, but I have worked hard to give my flock a happy and healthy life.

PSA: Owning a bird is not easy and I want to stress that anyone thinking of getting a bird should do plenty of research beforehand. I also encourage adopting from a rescue or ethical breeder rather than a chain pet store.

I started an instagram page to share pictures and videos of Shamu, and later Pebbles as well. I have loved sharing my flock with people and wanted to share them in a different way.

I started planning to create a children's book on Shamu years ago. I experimented with many different art styles.

Eventually, I decided on art that I felt highlighted the cuteness and playful side of Shamu.

I hope everyone enjoys this book and I invite you to follow us on instagram: **@shamuandpebbles**

Example of an old art style:

Meet the real life little bird named Shamu:

www.ingramcontent.com/pod-product-compliance
Lightning Source LLC
Chambersburg PA
CBRC090830120626
46547CB00008B/645